MARK HENRY

BY NICK GORDON

BELLWETHER MEDIA · MINNEAPOLIS, MN

Are you ready to take it to the extreme?
Torque books thrust you into the action-packed world
of sports, vehicles, mystery, and adventure. These books
may include dirt, smoke, fire, and dangerous stunts.
WARNING : read at your own risk.

Library of Congress Cataloging-in-Publication Data

Gordon, Nick.
 Mark Henry / by Nick Gordon.
     p. cm. -- (Torque: pro wrestling champions)
 Includes bibliographical references and index.
 Summary: "Engaging images accompany information about Mark Henry. The combination of high-interest subject matter and light text is intended for students in grades 3 through 7"--Provided by publisher.
 ISBN 978-1-60014-785-2 (hardcover : alk. paper)
 1. Henry, Mark, 1971---Juvenile literature. 2. Wrestlers--United States--Biography--Juvenile literature. I. Title.
 GV1196.H48G67 2012
 796.812092--dc23   2012000451

A special thanks to Devin Chen, Joh   ributing images.

CONTENTS

WARNING!

The wrestling moves used in this book are performed
by professionals. Do not attempt to reenact any
of the moves performed in this book.

TRIPLE THREAT CHAMP

Three of World Wrestling Entertainment's (WWE's) largest wrestlers stood in the ring. Mark Henry, Kane, and Big Show weighed a combined 1,156 pounds (524 kilograms)! The three were about to compete in a **Triple Threat match** for the Extreme Championship Wrestling (ECW) Championship. The bell sounded and the match began.

Wrestling Name: _ _ _ _ _ _ _ _ _ _ _ _ _Mark Henry

Real Name: _ _ _ _ _ _ _ _ _ _ _ Mark Jerrold Henry

Height: _ _ _ _ _ _ _ _ 6 feet, 4 inches (1.9 meters)

Weight: _ _ _ _ _ _ _ _ 412 pounds (187 kilograms)

Started Wrestling: _ _ _ _ _ _ _ _ _ _ _ _ _ _ _ 1996

Finishing Move: _ _ _ _ World's Strongest Slam

The three men battled back and forth for a long time. Eventually Big Show climbed to the top rope. Kane reached up and pulled him down to the mat. Both wrestlers were dazed, and Henry took advantage. He charged and leaped into the air. He landed on Kane. The referee counted Kane out and the match was over. Henry had won the championship!

BIG
SHOW

WHO IS MARK HENRY?

Mark Jerrold Henry was born on June 12, 1971 in Silsbee, Texas. At age 10, he weighed more than 200 pounds (91 kilograms). His size made him a star football player and weightlifter. He set three state records while on his high school **powerlifting** team. They were for the **bench press**, the **squat**, and the **deadlift**.

QUICK HIT!

Henry lifted 832 pounds (377 kilograms) when he set the record for the squat.

Henry competed at the 1992 and 1996 Olympics, but he did not win a medal. However, he earned gold, silver, and bronze medals at the 1995 Pan American Games. Many experts considered him to be the world's strongest man.

QUICK HIT!

Henry was named captain of the U.S. men's Olympic weightlifting team in 1996.

Henry joined WWE in 1996. He wrestled as a **face**. Henry was strong, but he lacked **technique**. WWE officials told him that he had to get into better wrestling shape. Henry eventually took a break from WWE to focus on powerlifting.

QUICK HIT!

Henry won the 2002 Arnold Strongman Classic. This earned him the official title of "World's Strongest Man."

BECOMING A CHAMPION

Henry returned to WWE in 2002. He suffered major leg and knee injuries over the next few years. He missed a lot of time while he recovered. In 2008, Henry beat Kane and Big Show to win the ECW Championship. He held the title for more than two months.

15

QUICK HIT!

In 2011, *Pro Wrestling Illustrated* named Henry the Most Improved Wrestler of the Year.

CHRISTIAN

In 2011, Henry attacked his teammates John Cena and Christian. He became a **heel**. In August of that year, he won a 20-man Battle Royal. This earned him a shot at the World Heavyweight Championship. A month later he defeated Randy Orton to claim the title.

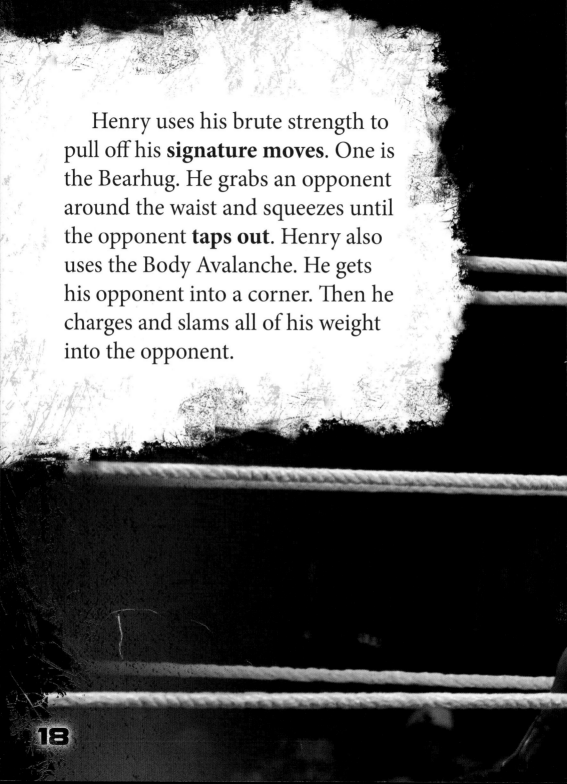

Henry uses his brute strength to pull off his **signature moves**. One is the Bearhug. He grabs an opponent around the waist and squeezes until the opponent **taps out**. Henry also uses the Body Avalanche. He gets his opponent into a corner. Then he charges and slams all of his weight into the opponent.

BODY
AVALANCHE

19

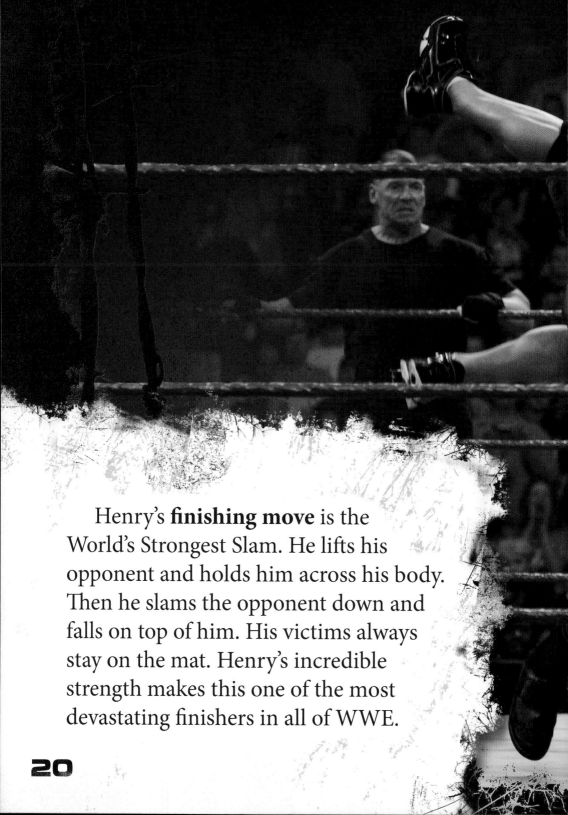

Henry's **finishing move** is the World's Strongest Slam. He lifts his opponent and holds him across his body. Then he slams the opponent down and falls on top of him. His victims always stay on the mat. Henry's incredible strength makes this one of the most devastating finishers in all of WWE.

WORLD'S STRONGEST SLAM

GLOSSARY

bench press—a powerlifting exercise in which a person lies flat on a bench and uses his or her arms to push a weighted bar upward

deadlift—a powerlifting exercise in which a person lifts a weighted bar off the ground from a crouched position

face—a wrestler seen by fans as a hero

finishing move—a wrestling move meant to finish off an opponent so that he can be pinned

heel—a wrestler seen by fans as a villain

powerlifting—a style of weightlifting that focuses on the bench press, squat, and deadlift

signature moves—moves that a wrestler is famous for performing

squat—a powerlifting exercise in which a person lifts a weighted bar on his or her shoulders and moves from a standing position to a squatting position

taps out—quits a match due to pain or injury caused by a submission hold

technique—skillful and proper performance of moves

Triple Threat match—a match in which three wrestlers fight at the same time; the first wrestler to pin either of his opponents wins the match.

TO LEARN MORE

AT THE LIBRARY

Black, Jake. *The Ultimate Guide to WWE*. New York, N.Y.: Grosset & Dunlap, 2011.

Kaelberer, Angie Peterson. *Cool Pro Wrestling Facts*. Mankato, Minn.: Capstone Press, 2011.

Stone, Adam. *The Big Show*. Minneapolis, Minn.: Bellwether Media, 2012.

ON THE WEB

Learning more about Mark Henry is as easy as 1, 2, 3.

1. Go to www.factsurfer.com.

2. Enter "Mark Henry" into the search box.

3. Click the "Surf" button and you will see a list of related Web sites.

With factsurfer.com, finding more information is just a click away.

INDEX